SPANISH BULL

- A Provocative Guide to Bullfighting -

MARK COLENUTT

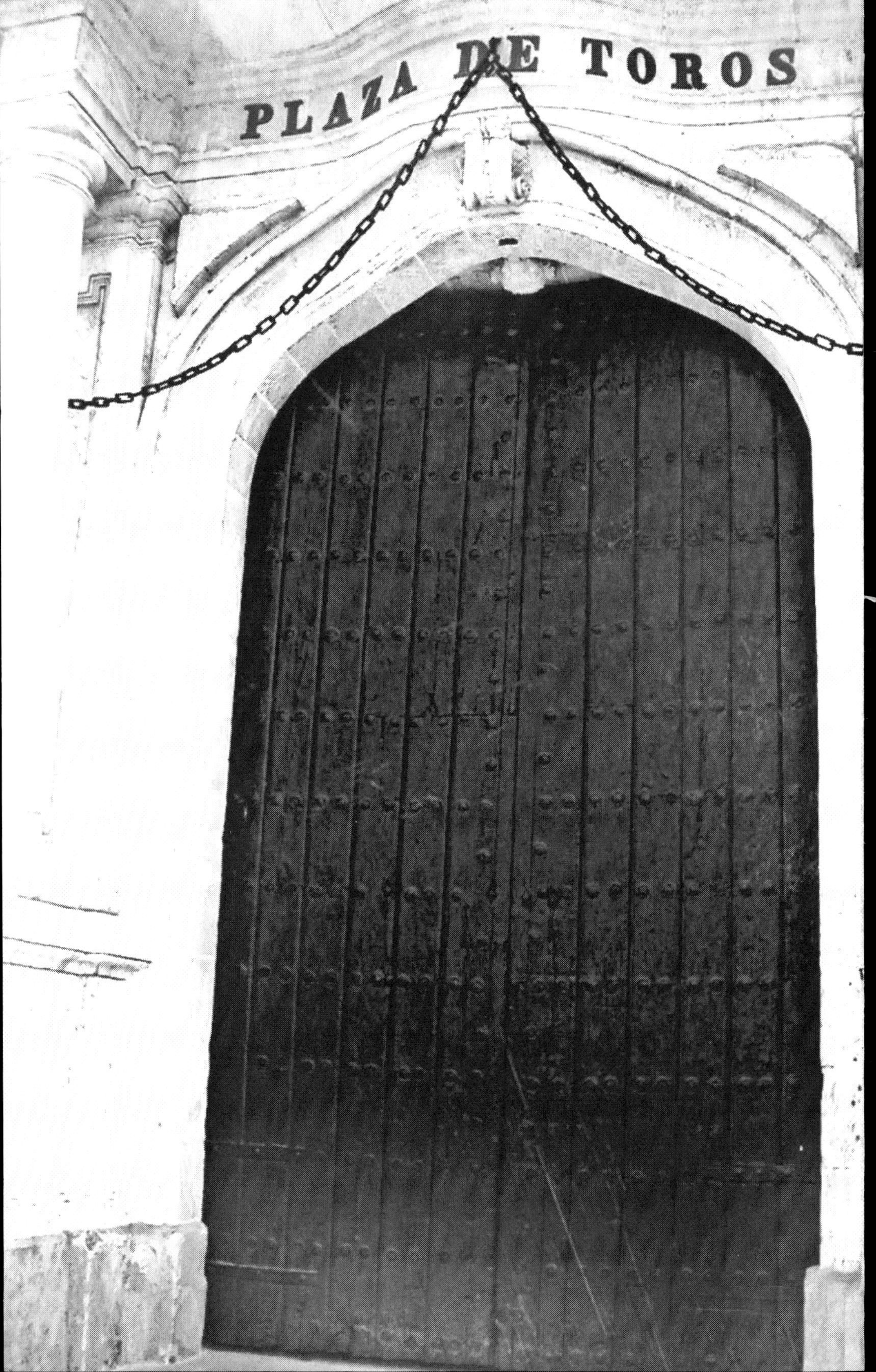
PLAZA DE TOROS

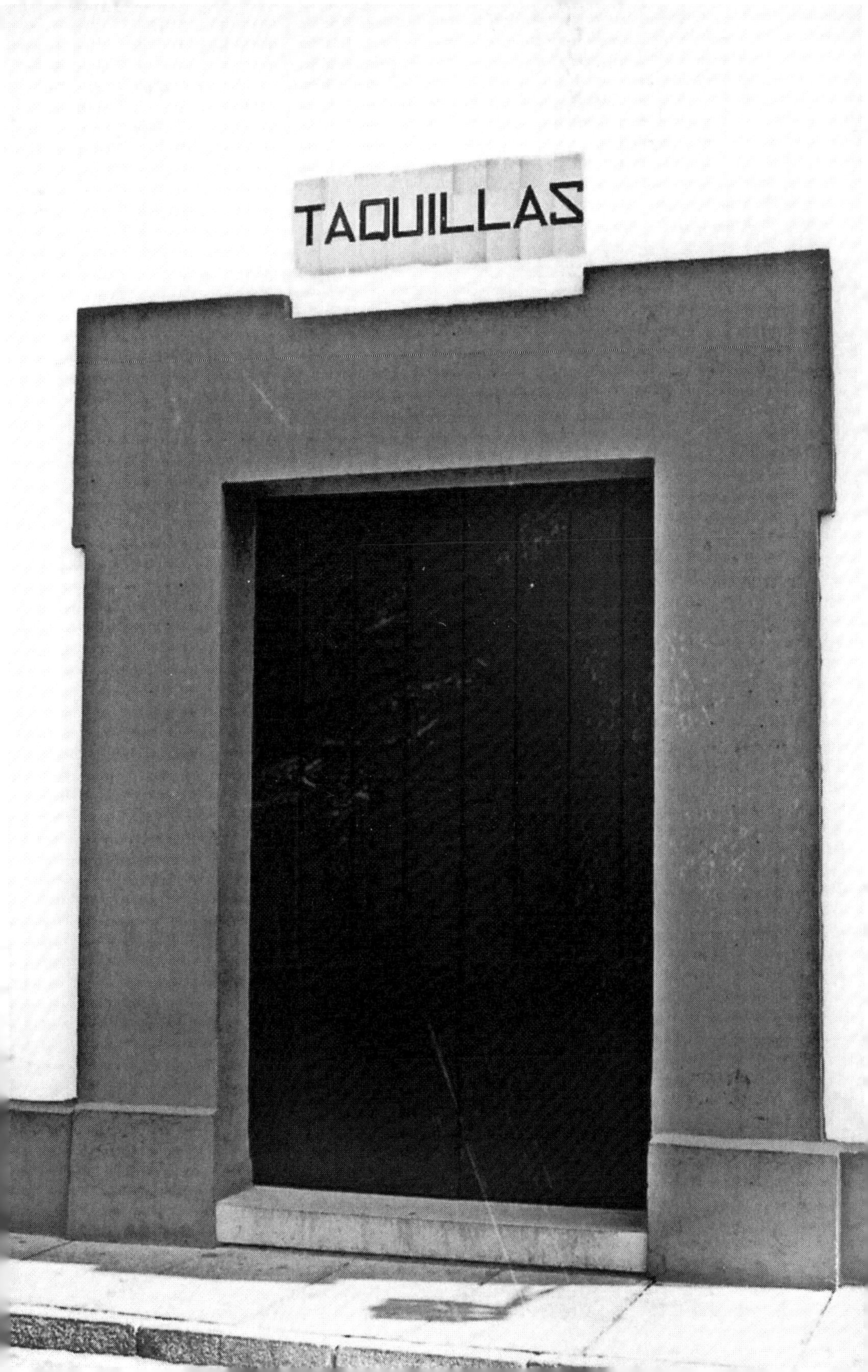
TAQUILLAS

Gilgamesh Books

Cover image: Giovanni Calia

ORÍGENES

'The composition of a tragedy requires testicles.'
Voltaire (1694-1778)

It is said by many of her citizens that Spain looks like an outstretched bull hide, which was its symbol for its 2002 European Presidency. And if Spain does indeed take this form then maybe it was preordained for Spain to be forever connected with the bull, which is just how the locals like it: fatalistic. Nowhere is this side of their psyche better seen than in the bullfight.

Going to the bullfight for the first time? Haven't a clue what it's all about? Going with a beautiful *señorita* or attractive *señor* and don't want to fail to impress? Eager to know what goes on behind the scenes and what the natives make of it all? Or perhaps, more to the point, you are simply culturally curious. The following then should be of some use.

Let's start at the beginning when primitive was all the rage. In the old days when stadiums were full of animals attacking each other as opposed to the spectacle being carried out by supporters, one of the stars of the show from earliest times was the bull. And with the bull being the symbol of the devil for some cultures, as well as a deity for others, this was an absolute must for the public. Bulls have been worshipped in many religions as symbols of potency and prized for their horns, which resemble the lunar crescent. The ancient auroch bulls were hunted and revered in Spain. Both the ancient Greeks and Basques believed that the first people were centaurs. In the ancient Near East and the Aegean, the wild auroch bull was extensively venerated as the Lunar Bull. It is quite typical for the god of one culture to be a demon in another. In many cultures the word 'cattle' also means 'money' or 'wealth'. These animals were one of the first and most exchangeable commodities. Hence a sacrificial calf was the most valuable offering that one could make. The killing of the bull here can therefore be seen as a confrontation with an evil spirit or equally as the sacrifice of a person's wealth.

The Romans were big on games and taking animals to their slaughter, so much so that they denuded great parts of North Africa of their fauna.

'Bull' in Spanish is *Toro* and the bullfight *'La Corrida de Toros'* is the only remnant of the Roman games we have with us in our modern era. It is a relic that has undergone a transformation leaving us only the original ring, a bull and a human pitted against an animal. The rest is all Hispanic even though it had once been all Latin.

Informally, it is simply referred to as: *'Los Toros'* - The Bulls. However, it is not called a 'bullfight' but a *'Corrida'*, literally meaning 'running'. *La Corrida* probably makes reference to the original chase, when bulls were hunted for purposes of entertainment. If it were strictly a fight then the bull would be killed as soon as possible, but it is not. Ironically in Pamplona, where they do run the bulls, it is not called a *Corrida;* but an *encierro,* from *encerrar* meaning to 'enclose'. They are run through the streets and then enclosed at their destination's end.

The title *'matador'* is used in Spanish but only in its full form: *'Matador de Toros'* - 'bullkiller'. The most commonly used name, however, is *Torero,* which has no direct translation and 'bullman' just doesn't have the same ring to it, no pun intended.

Next, one should know that it is not a 'sport' but an 'art'. One goes not to appreciate the killing as such, but more the manner in which it is achieved. If the *torero* does a good job it is referred to as a *buena faena*. The word *faena* is used in everyday language meaning – job or task, so it's a job well done.

'Bullfighting is the only art in which the artist is in danger of death and in which the degree of brilliance in the performance is left to the fighter's honor.'
Ernest Hemingway (1899-1961)

The bullfight as we know it didn't start to take shape until the 17th century in the ring at Ronda, a fine, classically colonnaded structure. Whether you like *La Corrida de Toros* or not, architecturally, it is well worth a visit. Ronda is believed by many to be the oldest *plaza* in Spain but that honour befalls *El Castañar* in Béjar c.1667, La Mancha. There is even an older structure in *la plaza de Las Virtudes* in Santa Cruz de Mudela, Ciudad Real. Curiously it isn't round but square and was built in 1643-5? but not used until 1722. The principal *plaza de toros,* however, is *Las Ventas* in Madrid. The capital, incidentally, has two *plazas de toros* the second is covered and is the pleasantly named *La plaza de Vistalegre.* If Spain is the bull's hide then Madrid is where its heart would have been but its soul is somewhere in the deep South of Andalucía.

Every *torero* wants to 'triumph' in Madrid; but curiously their dream is more than likely the desire to impress the crowd gathered in Sevilla (pronounced /se-VEE-ya/) during *La Feria de Abril. Los sevillanos* are regarded by their Spanish peers to be the most knowledgeable about the art.

Although Madrid is bullfighting HQ, it is Mexico City which possesses the world's largest ring with a seating capacity for some 55,000 *aficionados* in the Plaza Mexico arena. The oldest ring in the Americas is the *Plaza de toros de Acho* found in Lima, Peru and erected in 1776, which was rounded off even before the *La Maestranza* in Seville.

The Spanish Crown set up chivalric orders to encourage the nobles to train as horsemen, use weapons and be ready for action when called upon. *Las Reales Maestranzas* - Royal arsenals were formed, five in total. Together they formed the chivalric order known as *El Real Maestranza de Caballería* founded in the 17th century. Once their purpose had been served and fallen into disuse, as was the fate of Don Quixote, they turned their attentions to bullfighting and set up their respective rings. The five orders organized under Royal patronage are: Ronda, Sevilla, Granada, Valencia and Zaragoza. *La Real Maestranza de Caballería* in Sevilla (c.1671) doubles up as a benevolent institution offering scholarships for university studies, organizes fine arts competitions and historical publications. They also resolve social problems and help with the conservation of monuments. The Eldest Brother of the order is the King.

The *Maestranza* order demolished the original wooden bullring and made way for the present structure in 1758, which was completed in 1880. The bullring in Sevilla is not a perfect circle, as everyone here loves to tell visitors willing to lend an ear. Instead, it is more of an oval shape owing to the fact that they couldn't raze the town houses surrounding the ring. However, they created one of Spain's fairest structures, painted *'cal de Morón'* white, ringed in red with a yellow *albero* centre and able to seat up to 12,500 *aficionados*.

After Ronda it is possibly the most attractive bullring anywhere and it is strange that such a beautiful place has such a deadly purpose.

If you like a good argument then try and convince the locals it is a sport. To its many followers, *La Corrida* is an art - even a form of religious ritual.

> *"The bullfight is not a sport, it is a tragedy in three acts."*
> Orson Welles

Then there are those, even among its fans, who openly admit it is barbaric. The decision as to whether it is a sport, ritual or art is obviously a personal one. The lone brave Spaniard who dare voice an opinion contrary to their nation's eidolon counters the claim that it is an art form with the following assertion:

> *"Si la tauromaquia es una arte,*
> *entonces el canibalismo es gastronomía."*

(If bullfighting is an art, then cannibalism is gastronomy)

Hemingway and Orson Welles[1] were rhapsodic about the Spanish panoply of colour and found a meaning at every turn in the ceremonial death of the bull that no other walk of life could express.

---

[1] *Welles was a revered Hispanophile, whose special love of the country saw him buried there in Málaga, in the garden of a friend... in a well – what else?*

"Either you respect the integrity of the drama the bullring provides or you don't. If you do respect it, you demand only the catharsis which it is uniquely constructed to give."
Orson Welles

But it was the hispanophile French, who were responsible for projecting the present romantic image of the bullfight. Above all it was the Prosper Mérimée's story handed down to him by a gypsy that another Frenchman, Georges Bizet, transformed into the world's favourite opera, Carmen. The cigar curling *femme fatale* from Seville's gypsy quarter of Triana toyed with a soldier but she fell for a *torero*. Her statue stands half-hidden across from the *Maestranza* bullring near the Guadalquivir River.

In August 2004 RTVE, the government-owned TV and radio company, decided to halt transmission of the bullfight. Their motive, they said, was purely economical and not in any way political. However, the union of bull breeders believed the hand of animal rights activists was behind the decision. A spokesman for the union said, *"It has a political consequence that we completely reject for its contempt for a traditional and cultural manifestation of the highest magnitude and for its implications as a precedent reaffirming radical stances contrary to the fiesta."*

In August 2005 a scandal rocked the bullfighting world, which catapulted the debate into the spotlight. Claims of bribery, unfair treatment of bulls before they reached the ring and other backhand dealings caused a colossal stir. Many of the accusations were not new. Some bullfighters had even gone on record saying similar things had occurred at different times throughout their careers. Rumours that Vaseline has been used to blur the bull's vision and that horns have been shorn so the animal misjudges its distances when trying use them have been circulated for quite some time. What happened in August though was an *ex-torero* went on record and threw down all of these allegations in one go and the press lapped it up leaving the bullfighting fraternity momentarily lost for words.

This only encouraged the press to dig deeper. More than 20% of bulls analysed showed symptoms of having been drugged. Hearsay claims that weights are sometimes hung around the bull's neck for several weeks before the *Corrida* so the animal cannot lift its head high enough to defend itself properly. There has even been talk about animals being hit in the kidneys before taking to the *plaza*.

Spain's greatest living legend Curro Romero, from Camas in Sevilla, came out of retirement some years ago because he said the bulls were smaller and less dangerous than before. With *los Toros* now having become the domain of big money and handsome faces, perhaps the return to the old ways, which the purists have been crying out for, was about to happen.

Curro Romero

To underline the extent of support for the bullfight and the regard with which it is held, suffice to mention a singular incident, which took place in Sevilla in 1999 when a fight between a bar owner and his client broke out when disparaging comments were made about the illustrious *torero* Curro Romero. The altercation took place in Camas, the home town of the *matador de toros*. What was surprising though about the unique episode was that the judge found in favour of the bar owner who took to his fists first, summing up that the admiration in Camas was *"a way of understanding life."*

However, *la Corrida* does possess elements of display, victory, blood and sacrifice. Love or hate it, living in Spain and certainly old Seville you can't ignore it. It is an exhibition of colour and a pageant of music. It has an atmosphere and emotion that is heightened by a crowd's nervous expectations. The *Corrida's* age-old format of unpredictability where the destiny of the bull seems preordained could also prematurely seal the *torero's* fate. There is always the chance of an unexpected outcome. The victor is normally the *torero,* seldom the bull and almost always the paying public. Everyone loves a winner and so the public bask in the *torero's* defiance of death. The symbol of the blood apparently connects everything to the vitality of life, because buried deep in our psyches, red is the colour of imminent danger. Some look away, newbies may weep but the old faithful have become immune.

The despatching of the bull after its methodical preparation for the ring is a quasi-religious sacrifice, all made in Spain. The norm is to dedicate the bull to the President. However, if there is another dignitary present such as royalty then the *torero* will more than likely kill the bull in their honour. They won't kill it for their wife or mother, because it is rare that either is in attendance. They do not want to sit through the half-hour of torment waiting to see if their husband or son will finish the afternoon unscathed. It is not the winning that counts but the staying alive. But even coming out in one piece is seen as second best if the fighter hasn't demonstrated any valour in front of the bull and mastered its wild spirit. To kill and then walk away without having shown courage and contempt for your own possible demise will ensure any aspirant a very brief and fruitless career. Spain wants to see them confront man's worst fear with respect, control and passion by defying the frailty of our mortality and challenging the transience of our fleeting existence. Above all, they must take their time, take pleasure in the moment and overcome the danger by turning the fear into fascination as the 'artist' in the matador turns a possible death into a bold sword dance. Only after all that has been achieved may the *torero* truly say that he has *'triunfado'* in the ring.

The bullfight is a central part of any major Spanish celebration save *Semana Santa,* which is not a *fiesta. La Corrida* is called and regarded *"La Fiesta Nacional".* This in itself is at once credible and misleading. Some two million spectators attend the rings annually compared to five times that number who stagger into football stadiums. That is probably due to it not being so easy to kick a bull about. That said, the culture of the ring and sand is Spanish, while the pitch and its turf is an import. In 1991 *La Corrida* was given an official seal of approval when José Luis Corcuera, the then Interior Minister, passed the law *Ley de Espectáculos Taurinos* where, for the first time, it was classified officially as a *'cultural tradition'*. A tradition that apparently takes in around €750,000,000 a year and maintains 170,000 in employment. It is even subsidised in part by regional governments. Three times a week a bullfighting school congregates in Alamillo Park in Sevilla so its youngsters can practice their cape technique. The school is maintained through money from *La Junta de Andalucía* because the activity is seen as a Spanish cultural tradition that should be upheld. One could argue, why then in a land of writers and poets is not poetry subsidised as well?

Recently, events have accelerated the preservation or decline of the 'art form' when in July, 2010 the Catalan government, following a petition of 180,000 signatures, banned bullfighting in a heated debate, which saw the motion carried by 68 votes to 55. The act was politically charged as the prohibition was not just a move to protect animal rights but also an opportunity to uproot an undeniably Spanish cultural symbol from Catalan towns and cities. The truth of the matter was that the bullfight had all but withered away with most *plazas* having closed through inertia all over Catalunya. A ban was then in many respects a ceremonial formality. The most telling decision though, was the lack of action taken by the government to ban the *correbous*, popular in many towns in southern Catalunya.

A single bull is unloaded from a lorry with a rope tied to its horns from where it is cajoled and heckled as it begins its route into town. There, it is tied to a pillar, its horns adorned with torches, which are then set ablaze. The popular summer *fiestas* which occur in the municipalities south of Tarragona were enshrined in Catalan law by 114 votes to 14 to protect the tradition, just two months after the Catalan government in Barcelona had banned bullfighting. The claim that *correbous* is typically Catalan does not hold water either, as it is also typical in Andalucía. If animal rights had really been the central issue then the *correbous* should have been retired along with the bullfight. Obviously then, while torture is abhorrent torment is considered fair entertainment.

In reaction, in part, to the decision of Catalunya against bullfighting the Spanish government in November, 2013 moved to preserve the national *fiesta* in law and thereby set aside public funds to promote and protect the centuries-old pageant. The act of parliament came in response to a 600,000 signed petition (one of the signatories was the Nobel winning author Mario Vargas Llosa) and the law afforded *La Corrida* national cultural heritage status. It remains to be seen if the legislation by the central government will take precedence over the decision of the regional Catalan government and thereby reinstate the bullfight there, which many hope it will.

The first Spanish region to ban bullfighting though wasn't Catalunya but the Canaries in 1991 and no such cultural conflict of identities occurred.

La Corrida alludes to national qualities of bravery, pride, unity and euphoria as well as a potent Spanish cocktail of folklore, superstition and religion. It is an age-long popular event that not only ties Spain to her past but also keeps it mindful of its future, as does any tradition. So there can be no living icon more symbolic than a Spanish singer or dancer who has married a *torero*. There are several of these couples in Spain, who receive their due attention and blessing from the people. Byron wrote in Don Juan that:

> *All tragedies are finish' d by a death.*
> *All comedies are ended by a marriage.*

That is the art of it, but what of its lineage?

SUN & *SOMBRAS*

The rest of the *La Corrida de Toros* should be unfolded *paso a paso;* that is step by step. We will look at the hard facts, history and traditions that go into its make-up.

The full name of the Spanish bull is *Toro Bravo,* meaning 'brave bull'. The bulls that actually go into the ring (not all of them meet the grade) are called *Toros de Lidia,* 'fighting bulls'. The bull is labelled as 'brave' because, although it is punished in the ring with pain, it will keep on charging. Most bulls would shy away after the first experience of it.

By the 16th century, there were established bull breeders called *ganaderos,* and the *Corrida* had survived as the most popular element of the ancient world's bloodthirsty games. A century later and the *toro bravo,* as we know him today, began to take shape with the first 'official' bloodline: *La Jijona.* A hundred years on and the four main bloodlines were formed: *Raíz Cabrera, Gallardo, Raíz Vázquez* and *Raíz Vistahermosa,* just like the 'pure' bred English racehorse that can be traced back to one of three Arab stocks. The Spanish bull, as all domestic European cattle, is descended from the now extinct auroch *(Bos Taurus primigenius.)* The last known example perished in a Polish park in 1627.

Today the principal areas that breed bulls are the provinces of Toledo, Salamanca and of course the region of Andalucía where the bull populates some of the most remote areas of Europe. One reason given for many that support *La Corrida* is that the animal lives well. Those that are kept as studs can live up to 20 years and in a season will mate on average four times a day with a herd of some 45 females. A bull is free to roam but then again the countryside is also a breeding ground for flies and mosquitoes that will pester the bull until he enters the ring.

Before a year of his life has passed, he is rounded up, separated from his mother and branded. Here, across the extensive Andalusian plains and expansive skies, come charging

Western Europe's first and only cowboys - *vaqueros*[2], with lances in hands and the long manes of their Spanish horses dancing in the breeze. The riders gallop close as they try to separate cow from calf. The cow is quicker than her bull-calf, more agile and more determined. The lance - *la garrocha,* serves to knock the calf over by hitting its hindquarters as it turns. This running down of the bullock and then bringing him to ground is known as *acoso y derribo* and competitions in this discipline are held all over Andalucía. The rider, in flat cap and side-burns, draws the cow away from the young bull. When they finally trap him and take him to be branded, it is the last time the mother will see him. As the calf is immobilised and awaits his initiation, a large bonfire keeps the breeder's branding irons 'on ice'. As the initials and numbers are burnt in, the bull obviously cries out in pain.[3] When all is done it is everyman for himself. The bull, now on its feet, wants to exact revenge. From the very moment the animal can stand properly it is prepared to charge anything. With good reason it takes its frustration out on the only thing that has remained behind and runs its horns through the centre of the fire scattering it in all directions.

---

[2] *In origin the cowboy is from the Spanish south and anything but an American original. The only place in Europe where cattle have been herded on horseback for centuries is Andalucia and it was the Spanish that exported this system to the New World. Hence 'cowboy' is a translation from the Spanish 'vaquero' and not vice-versa.*

[3] *This obvious point is relevant when considering the claim of some scientific studies which have determined that the bull does not experience pain in the ring due to its high adrenalin levels.*

Over time the selection process has bred the bull we are familiar with today. So familiar is the breed that we even know the characteristic 40ft high silhouette from the Osborne sherry bottles and the great images the company has dotted around the Andalusian countryside to advertise itself. They used to be seen in there hundreds but now only 97 survive, which started life in 1956 to promote their cognac. These remaining profiles have been declared a national monument after the Supreme Court ruled in 1997 that the bull sign: *"enhances the view rather than encourages consumption."* As the Spanish novelist Julio Llamazares observed, *"this was because, like mountains, castles, and villages, the bulls were landmarks. After seeing them for so many years beside our roads, after embracing them as part of our collective and individual iconography, it was hard to imagine life without them."*

Not all the bulls are black of course, though they do carry the same horns, broad shoulders and neck that even Mike Tyson would have envied. The *Miura,* the most feared 'man-killer' tends to be light grey. This breed from Andalucía has slain more *toreros* than any other. Some are skewbald, others sorrel, many are dun in colour as well as roan. Times change even in such traditional institutions and today's most unpredictable breed is the *Victorino Martín. Miuras* have declined as *toreros* have refused to face them. Maybe they will be pacified or the breeder could be out of business. As the bullring has changed from the refuge of the working man to the arena of the gentry, bulls have, according to the well-informed, reduced in size and ferocity.

In order to look for the right characteristics in an animal that will be chosen for the ring they test the cow, not the bull-calf. If she, under 'light' punishment, continues to charge the mounted horseman then she is deemed to have *casta,* which is the 'determined spirit' and breeding that defines the bull in its relentless attack to defend itself against an aggressor. This trial and selection process is called *La Teinta.* From the mother comes courage and the father just bestows his good looks. His broad shoulders hold up an immense pack of bulging neck muscle and the back tapers down to narrow haunches. The forehead is squared, as is the formation of the horns that turn out from the temple at right angles to face anything which is foolish enough to cross its path. It is awkward when seen from its flank but when admired head-on its stance is that of a seated sovereign in audience: noble, dominant and unmistakably potent. There is no sign of danger from this apparently placid bovine. It does not roar, bare teeth nor rear up. Above all, what draws the viewer in, is the abyss of its black eyes. Dark as the night and soulless in their sinister emptiness, its eyes are as penetrating as its horns. It can seem serene in posture, wearing an expression of indifference, which at its most innocent verges on inquisitiveness, but all this changes the moment it charges.

Once passed *la teinta,* the bull born into this world is branded, tagged and named for posterity. From then on, it is left for anything from 3 to 6 years to live the good life during which time it must not experience any cape play nor be near a man on foot. That is why those who work in the country with the bulls do so on horseback. This is done not just for the obvious reason of getting away quicker but so the bull does not learn to charge the man instead of the cape.

Three-year-old bulls are taken for novice bullfighters - *novilleros,* and the six-year olds, wise with age, are chosen for *toreros* wearing full colours. The day a *novillo* finally becomes a fully fledged *torero* is called '*tomando la alternativa*'. A bull may look like a dumb animal but it is an incredibly fast learner when it comes to working out who or what the real danger is: the cape or its carrier? This knowledge on the part of the bull is called *sentido* - sense. On average it takes 15 minutes to kill a bull in the *Corrida* and woe betide the man who takes any longer. During a bull's tragic 15 minutes of fame some do actually figure out who to go for and then the *torero* realises they are in trouble. However, if a bull has received any cape play before getting into the ring it is an experience the animal never forgets. Then the man and not the cloth will be the animal's target from the very start of *la corrida*.

Capeas are 'anyone-can-have-a-go' *corridas* using experienced animals - often cows - *vaquillas* - which move faster. *Las capeas,* are usually held in summer during local *fiestas,* and are attended by many participants. This is when the casualty list is set to soar. One bull was taken from *capea* to *capea* and gored its way through over 60 lives until it was eventually sent out to pasture. *Encierros* are also another central part of many a local *fiesta* in both northern and southern Spain. From the verb *encerrar* meaning 'to enclose', this is the famed running of the bulls from a pen through pinched streets into the *plaza de toros.* Again, they are also common in summertime. The oldest is to be found in the town of Cuéllar to the province of Segovia and dates back over 500 years. The bulls are followed on horseback, run through a pine forest, then into open plains and finally through the centre of town.

The bullfight did not begin life on foot but on horseback and such a form still exists and it is called *Rejoneo* in reference to the pole - a *rejón*, which is used to stab the bull while mounted on a horse. Andalusian riders sit astride grand armchair-like Portuguese saddles and their horses sport glistening manes tied back with interwoven ribbons. The horsemen don the short jacket of the *vaquero* and what must be the world's most intricate chaps - *sajones*, strapped to their legs. The Domecq family that own the French-founded sherry *bodega* of Domecq in Jerez de la Frontera in the province of Cádiz are the most notorious on the *Rejoneo* circuit. The horses are piebald, bay, jet black or snow-white in colour. These agile mounts have been trained to respond without thinking and are as faithful and sure as any police dog. One moment's hesitation would cost horse and rider dear.

The riders are referred to as *rejoneadores* and obviously, because of cost, there are few of them about. Each rider takes several horses with them, all of which make an appearance during an afternoon's display.

In Portugal the *Rejoneo* has reached a more refined level than in Spain, a fact the Spanish bullfighting fraternity openly admit. The Portuguese tend use the Lusitano horse known for its bravery and is the oldest mounted horse in history with 5,000 years of riding under its saddle. However, the present breed probably began to take shape after the invading Moors mixed the Iberian horses with their Barb warhorses. It is very similar to the Andalusian horse, which is also referred to as the Pure Spanish Horse. Both breeds went their separate ways in 1966 when defined lines of strain were established. What also sets the Portuguese *Rejoneo* apart from its Spanish derivation is that they don't kill the bull. They do, however, place tipped darts in its neck muscles, so while not sacrificed it is still harmed.

The equestrian bullfight dates as far back as 13th century. The *Rejoneo,* meant only for aristocrats, remained unchanged in both Portugal and Spain until the end of the 18th century, when Carlos II (1665-1700) of Spain died without an heir. The throne then passed to a grandson of Louis IV, who became Felipe V

(1700-1748), and so the Bourbon dynasty entered Spain along with their French influence and disdain for bullfighting. The Bourbons prohibited the *fiesta nacional*. While the decree was adhered to by the governing class it was rejected by the common people and the bullfighters took to their feet leaving their horses behind. It wasn't until 1920 that *el Rejoneo* was again seen in Spain.

The process of training a horse for the *plaza* is a complicated one and in order to get the handful of horses they need they will buy anything up to a hundred just so they can extract two or three that will eventually confront a fully grown bull, but not after years of training first. What they do with the rest of the horses is anyone's guess. It is a costly business and so *el rejoneo* is not for the financially faint hearted.

The last Sunday of *La Feria de Abril,* the great April Fair of Sevilla, is traditionally *El Rejoneo* in the morning, but you'll have to be early. The traditional *Corrida* on foot pulls more of a crowd because there is more risk. And in Spain, at times, if there is no risk involved there is no point in doing anything. Risk taking is in the blood here, hence the running of the bulls in village *fiestas* and pedestrians taking their lives into their own hands, when crossing the road, always seeing just how close they can get to the passing cars. The last Sunday afternoon of Sevilla's *Feria* is always reserved for the notoriously unpredictable Miura bulls, thus leaving the best to last.

In the noteworthy town of Ronda, set over an impressive gorge between Sevilla and Málaga, is one of Spain's most picturesque bullrings. Each year in September they celebrate a 'Goyaesque' *Corrida* in homage to the local born *torero* Pedro Romero (1754-1839), who created the classical style of bullfighting. *La Corrida Goyesca de Ronda* takes place during the week-long *Feria de Pedro Romero*. The bullfighters dress in typical 18th century costume and recreate the atmosphere faithfully captured by the Spanish painter Goya, whose famous sketches are in El Prado in Madrid. There is one notable exception to the sketches and that is there is goring of horses in the ring, unless a bull successfully upends a picador's mount.

In Portugal it is also typical to see the *rejoneador* always dressed in period long coat and frilled shirt. Another typical sight at a Portuguese *Rejoneo* are the *Forcados*. A group of unpaid men, who jump into the ring in unison and entertain the crowd by receiving the charging bull head on in a *pega de cara* - loosely translated as 'a slap in the face.' They have to wrestle the *toro* to a stand-still. They come into the ring when the *rejoneador* has finished with the bull. (In Portugal they don't kill it, remember) The team of men was originally employed to stop the bull from running up a staircase which linked the Royal box to the bullring. They had a *forcado* lance to repel the bull. They still carry the *forcado* when they enter the ring in the *paseíllo*. Broken bones are the norm for these elf-dressed bull tamers.

On the select day of a *Corrida* the bull, if it hasn't already been seriously wounded, lost an eye, or even killed in a tussle in the field, will be moved by using steers into a box and transported to the ring. Six bulls are required for each *Corrida* and one is kept in reserve in case one fails to charge in the ring. Sometimes a further bull is also taken. Early morning the bulls are off-loaded into a *corral* where they are inspected by a vet looking for physical defects that would in any way inhibit them from playing their full part in the proceedings.

Following the inspection there is a *sorteo* where lots are drawn for the bulls. They are divided into the three best and the three worst and then paired off, one from each group. The names of pairs are then picked out of a hat by either the *toreros'* managers, *los apoderados,* or one of their assistants who will also be in the ring with them that afternoon. Once that is done, the bulls are arranged in order through a complex system of gates and channelling and there they remain until their time comes.

The bulls have reached the final stage and within a few hours they will each take their turn in the *plaza* with their respective *matador de toros* and an expectant, paying public. Here the *aficionados* - impassioned followers, will decide if the bull brought before them is 'keen', *celoso,* or *codicioso* if he runs in straight lines and therefore easier to manage but still up for the challenge. However, if he does not take to the *plaza* in the expected spirit and does not engage the *torero* properly, then he is *manso,* either cowardly or no good. Occasionally the problem is the bull's hooves do not support his weight properly and they fold as he turns. This has its own phrase in Spanish: *se doblan las manos.* In such cases the bulls are usually removed.

The day for the *torero* begins with the ritual of dressing, a process that takes up to an hour. Each *traje de luces,* 'suit of lights' (if one can translate it as that), costs in excess of €7,000 and is carefully laid out before each garment is put on. Here the rite becomes evident. The fine line between escaping unscathed or receiving a goring and at worst, death, is often luck. This tends to persuade even the least superstitious not to tempt fate and obsessive behaviour patterns become the norm. The suit is arranged in the same way for each event before the *torero* enters his dressing room, which is usually the hotel room. It is put on in the same order each time and then prayers and talismans are addressed. Superstition, religion and providence are called upon and respected. There is no apparent irony in the mixing of the three elements here; they are all one in the same trinity. Where once there may well have been humour there are now only nerves. The trousers, called *taleguilla,* are possibly the most important part of the costume, so tight that not even the slightest wrinkle appears in the silk fabric. Loose fitting material could easily be hooked by a horn, carrying the wearer with it. The stockings are always pink and the slippers are dainty looking but supposedly good for grip, except in rain.

The frilled shirt is fronted by a thin tie harking back to those worn by the Mods. The jacket, heavily adorned with gold motif, is open in the underarm to allow greater mobility. It is made of silk but is as hard as board. Only the *torero* is permitted the gold on his jacket and trousers. The *picador*, the mounted horseman whose job it is to spike the bull in the neck during the *Corrida*, is the only one to have gold trim on his hat. The *torero's* 'team' in the ring, called *cuadrilla*, wear silver or black motif.

A false circular pigtail called *coleta* is attached to the back of the head, reminiscent of those worn by Roman gladiators. On the day of a *torero's* retirement the *coleta* is symbolically cut off.

A *torero's* greatest area of exposure is the inner thigh where a major artery runs. A goring here is the most common form of fatality. The blood loss can be so great at times that they are lifeless by the time they reach the infirmary inside the bullring. Padding is usually placed here to add some reassurance, if little else. However, for the first time spectator, the exaggerated bulge may lead some innocents to believe that such manhood is a prerequisite for entering the ring. As any Spaniard will be only too pleased to exclaim, the bravery is actually in the balls - apparently: *Hay que tener cojones*. A goring is referred to as a *cornada*, from *cuerno* meaning 'horn'. Here if you have horns though - *tienes cuernos*, or someone 'has given you horns' - *te han puesto los cuernos*, then your partner has been unfaithful. The symbolism, however, has nothing to do with bulls.

SPANISH BULL

Once everything else is in place the hat, *montera,* is donned. After praying and walking to the ring the three *toreros* of the afternoon, who will each face two bulls, wrap themselves up in an exquisitely embroidered cape - *capote de paseo,* which may well bear the image of their patron saint. They are now ready to face what destiny has in store for them. Such allusions made to fate and fortune are no small matter here. Not only in the ring but right across the land that makes up Spain, fate pervades the attitude of the people. The national lottery here is not just about winning to be rich. Every slight piece of luck that comes your way gains you status here. People's eyes widen when they hear of your good turn no matter how small. Death is out in the arena and somewhere with it is Fate deciding whether today she will be kind or not.

On 26th September, 1984 in the small town of Pozoblanco, Spain's most popular *torero* of the hour, Francisco Rivera Pérez, known as *'Paquirri',* was gored by the bull *'Avispado'* from the breeders *Sayalero y Brandés* and bled to death in the infirmary while the television cameras recorded the whole gruesome spectacle of the man's fading moments. One of the other *toreros 'El Yiyo'* on the afternoon's bill was also killed in *la plaza* some years later, gored through the heart. The third, *'El Soro',* after turning badly in the ring broke his ankle and could never return to the profession. The promoter of that fatal afternoon in Pozoblanco was also killed in a car accident soon afterwards.

These incidents all have rational explanations but here the people talk of a cursed bill-poster. It is tradition that when a *torero* is killed in the *plaza* then the bull's body is burnt and his mother is sacrificed. The body burning could be for superstition but the killing of the mother is to ensure that a bloodline capable of killing once won't go on to seize a *torero* twice. They like their bulls brave but not deadly. When one of Paquirri's *cuadrilla* of that afternoon learned that the head of the bull that had killed the *torero* had not been burnt but instead mounted and displayed in the bar *Hermanos Lora* in Gelves, Sevilla, he was shocked into silence. Superstition plays a very real part in and out of the *plaza*.

It has been known on occasion to *indultar* the bull, where it isn't killed because either the *torero* or the public feel that the animal has never let up, always taken the cape *'siempre va al trapo'* as they say, and is therefore *noble*. The *cabestros* – tame oxen, are released into the ring and the bull follows them out.

SOL
TENDID

BARRERAS 1ª. FILA
2ª. ,,
3ª. ,,

BAJO

S 8-10

L 138   AL 172
  140   ,, 174
  142   ,, 178

HORNS & TAILS

- TWO ENDS OF A BULL -

Here it would be constructive as well as appropriate to invoke the two extreme and opposing views concerning bullfighting by breathing new life into the time-worn prejudices that the author has heard for several decades:

- HORNS -

On extensive ranches owned by self-important landlords fatter than the terrain they have possessed through privilege, they have modelled themselves as the seated aristocracy, tightening their circles and heightening their status. Here they breed the bull that stands as the central symbol of their national identity and as a result, they have a perceived responsibility as guardians against those within and without to preserve it.

They play central fiddle on a national stage and through their protagonism exercise a cultural control on a people's imagination and perception of themselves. Without them Spain would be foreign.

However, the bulls they breed go to the slaughter as many animals did before them in the games organised by the Romans. But the Romans offered no introspection, dissection of culture or higher motives. This was simply killing as entertainment.

Nevertheless, if anything can last long enough it will naturally obtain a thick coat of history, cultural connections and a background of philosophy to its changed status. Over the years with the addition of other cultural influences such as the Moors, for example, laid over the previous influence of earlier occupiers, these influences connected with the adornment of Catholic iconography, which revolutionised the ritual procedure of taking bulls into a ring and sacrificing them for a spectator's cheap thrill. The killing of the bull, of religious significance to the pagans before the lamb was taken up by the Christians, has taken on a more popular role in society.

The mob intoxicates itself on a centuries-old fix of morbid exhibition. Just as modern American games depend on cheerleaders, hype and music, so the bullring is alive with similar peripheral adornment such as music bands that fill the air with *paso dobles*, vibrant colours, elaborate clothing, accentuated ritual and its new found life as a catwalk for socialites. The flags of *Andalucía*, Sevilla and the Austrian colours which are also those of the Maestranza bullring fly high in the afternoon sun as the music filters across rooftops and can easily be heard from the *azoteas* in Triana and the balconies in *calle Betis* on the other side of the river.

Take away the 'glitz' and we are left with someone who just wants to kill an animal while taking risks to win the favour of the public. It has therefore changed very little in essence over time. Today the man is on foot as opposed to mounted; he's decoratively dressed; adored if successful and rejected if not. What have come of age are its study and the pretence of knowledge that has come to surround it. The philosophising and the weight given it by adoring *aficionados* has lent it an air of officialdom, false intelligentsia, unapparent wisdom and an intricateness that is hidden from the uninitiated. It thereby creates an enlightened elite to be envied as opposed to those that have not had the privilege to be initiated. Do not let ourselves be deceived here by trimmings and carefully judged processes designed to heighten the emotions and over look suffering. The bull has been dressed in Devil's clothing and the conscience despatched by morbid social acceptability. So, for a brief moment we may give flight to our darker and more damaging nature in the wider world of our own moral abyss. Eloquent and exciting words on the sense of life is intensified by *'being closer to death'* may dance a delight on your ear but a living creature's blood has drenched the ground for you to feel such short-lived titillation. If we, as a species, ever wish to attain permanent peace in our world then we must first do battle with our negative and blood thirsty instincts and not try to co-exist happily with them by convincing ourselves that they are anything other than what they are: self-destructive.

Great part of man's failing in maintaining its hard won civilisation is directly linked to this ever continuing self-deception that such brutality and violence can be explained away and draped in acceptability. Death is invoked for pleasure as war is waged for glory.

From the same point of view but looking at the subject matter more starkly, a more passionate voice could claim that a fattened bull breeder lords it over the rest of us while bragging to those bored enough to listen of how his bulls are the biggest, bravest blah, blah, blah. On some false ego-trip no doubt. This Brylcreemed, striped shirt, cigar smoking, status driven parody of insecure snobbery sells these animals to a man lacquered with even more Brylcreem®, an even greater collection of stripy shirts, but with no need for the cigars. This individual is vainglorious and derives his eminence from dressing up like a glittery figurine and then after deliberately debilitating the animal beforehand by mortally wounding it, he then prances around a ring cheered on by a bloodthirsty public lead by the mob instinct eager to feed a frenzy for cruelty. They channel their own impulses out of themselves by attacking the bull, which symbolises some oppressive dark force: namely death. This sequined, pink-stockinged, slipper wearing, tight-trousered male (supposedly an icon of male virility) kills bulls, makes a lot of money and then defends his interests, as you can imagine anyone making a fair penny would, in the name of 'art' and 'culture'.

We all know that the people are there for the voyeuristic pleasure of watching a blood-spectacle like the gruesome reality TV shows that encourage us to laugh at the horrors of accidents and untransmittable acts of human brutality. But because this is only an animal we let it go by and dress it up respectably so we can parade it out before the masses and allow those who indulge their more sinister nature to appear to be on a higher plain of cultural susceptibility. The irony is almost tangible while the blood and suffering is complete and the joy in the stands arguably sickening.

- TAILS -

'Italy' may mean 'land of the bull' but it is Spain (which incidentally comes from the Carthaginian word 'Isphan' meaning 'land of the rabbit') where the animal has been truly immortalised in its earthly moment of high drama. In a Europe ever increasingly mechanised, controlled and a consumerism dependant on social struggle lusting for status, we have perhaps lost meaning to our daily existence and alienated ourselves from our natural needs. Our attention has been diverted and a series of pursuits, which benefit those at the top of the business chain, put in their place.

Life is followed by quietus, try as we might in our industrial lives to distance ourselves from this fact. It is in the bullfight that we find Europe's last vestige of man facing death defiantly for glory and the greater good of a people that witness this act of faith, bravery and desperate drama of the frailty of life. The Indians hold the cow sacred, while the Spanish attach their insecurity to the bull. If they can defeat the bull in an ephemeral afternoon, they can at least look their last hour in the eye and have the upper hand. While all this is played out the rest of the Western, self-dubbed 'civilised' world, watches on in horror, frustrated that there is something beyond their control.

In an age-old custom the bulls are bred on the land as the matadors come up through the ranks and both are finely tuned by traditional wisdom and technique until they finally meet on the nation's stage in *la fiesta nacional*, in *la corrrida*, where centuries of a people's culture come to bear upon one man's shoulders. For one afternoon he becomes death, the destroyer of bulls where death begets death. And by the close of the *fiesta* life will continue with renewed vitality having felt mortality and acknowledged its presence among us. Here the moribund moment becomes a material entity and through the *torero* we have the opportunity to confront it. The bullring has handed down to us a perennial element of the religions of the ancients, which teaches us that with our departure from this world there also arrives life, which is an ongoing resurrection and not some future event.

The ritual, risk and religion are not for those preoccupied by petty social one-upmanship. You must go within yourself and beyond, away from your TVs and 9 to 5s to find a deeper meaning to what surrounds you. Where will you be in 100 years? What emotions will you have experienced in your lifetime? And where will they have taken you?

Then all of a sudden you find yourself alone, a bull staring into you and you begin to perceive the natural forces that preside over our man-made illusion. *La Corrida* brings this stark reality to bear.

Man kills animals for sporting pleasure, whether it be hunting or fishing. Man kills animals for eating delight and not simply as a means of survival. In our modern world, is it essential to eat meat to meet our protein requirements? What of the life of our bovine herds that are factory bred and raised in an industrial process? Is this an expressive 'meaningful' life for an animal that gives up its life for us? No animal-rights activist can agree to this.

Now contrast this with the existence of the *toro bravo*. Born into this world they awake in the *dehesa* - the uncultivated meadowlands of southern Spain and some of Western Europe's last wilderness. They are kept well-fed and cared for and more importantly left to roam the landscape until they are called upon. Instead of being crammed into a lorry and then dragged into an abattoir that reeks of death to be shot, six of them are led to a ring where they are given the chance to end their days as their nature dictates: as a fighting bull. They are given the exclusive prospect to face their executioner, which no factory animal ever has. More often than not they go down fighting, but a brave few get to walk away.

No meat eater then, can ever criticise the bullfight and the way the *toro bravo* is treated, as the acute hypocrisy would only belie their glaring lack of common sense. To even begin to argue against *la Corrida*, you must first give up meat.

If we were to make an analogy on a human level we can see that there is a marked difference between cramming people into a slaughterhouse to be butchered and pushing a Goliath into an arena to face a David to fight for his life. If you had to choose, which path would you elect? Perhaps then the salient point of the debate under this light is not so much how the animal is killed, but rather that people pay to watch the macabre scene. But then people pay for the pleasure of eating meat. If this is not the case then there is no explaining the viral invasion of burger joints the world over, which people turn to in their leisure time. And yet do people go to watch the killing or to sense the drama of the moment? Only in the *plaza* is the bull is given a chance to fight for his life. There is no other instance where livestock is given the option of seizing their liberty by slaying their captor.

From the same point of view, but looking at the subject matter more starkly, a more passionate voice could claim that those who oppose the bullfight most fervently are the sort of people unable to connect properly with other humans. They believe animals are superior to humans, only because an animal never answers them back. Who would keep a cat or dog for long if the animal argued with them? The animal's passive nature is what makes it acceptable to pet lovers. People have to be respected on all levels especially when their opinions are unpalatable. Animal lovers do not have to compromise themselves with such complex emotions; they merely speak and their pet listens and apparently willingly obeys.

Many eat meat but decry animal mistreatment. Where is the sense in that? They want all species to survive, but without the bullfight the *toro bravo* would cease to do precisely that. Who will look after the bulls? Those that make the loudest noise will be the most silent when it comes to preserving these magnificent beasts for posterity. They are too prepossessed in their urban lifestyles. And this is where they hail from, from the artificial construct of polite suburbia, far removed from any rural reality. They have, for as long as their social memory can conjure, been devoid of dealing with death on a regular basis. It was as if Disney held some greater truth for them as to the essence of existence than any direct contact with the creation and loss of life as a daily part of our subsistence. The bullfight therefore unnerves them and jolts them awake from their innocent cartoon-derived vision of a world that only exists in a celluloid daydream.

Try as we might life is not the *couleur de rose* we are desperate to find it to be. It has its cruel nature and we deceive ourselves if we hide ourselves from it. We destroy millions of animals every year, hidden from view and then dress the remains in appealing packaging in order to mask over death. Supermarket shoppers, who have never witnessed a *matanza,* when an animal is slaughtered, somehow believe they are in a position to pass sentence on the bullfight, but what inverted arrogance is this? It is that of a child disparaging a hard-working parent for not buying all they want for Christmas.

For suburbia to live out their cotton wool-coated fancy, they must depend on the rural community to supply them with sustenance. So, before they take the moral high ground they should step down from their Spanish castle in the sky and sample life as Mother Nature intended on the land and then they will first better understand, and can then evaluate, their 'naturalistic' philosophy on life.

DEATH IN
THE AFTERNOON

Entering the *plaza* the *toreros* process in behind two horsemen, *alguaciles,* dressed in 16th century period cloaks with striking feathered caps. Traditionally these bailiffs cleared the ring of spectators but have remained for ceremonial purposes. They also act as the President's representatives in the *plaza*. Walking out through the entrance they parade towards the President's box high up above the main exit gate. This precursor to the main event is known as the *paseíllo,* from the word *paseo* - a stroll. On the President's right, as he looks out onto the *plaza,* will be the senior *torero* - in rank not age - to the left the number two seed of the afternoon. Last, and in this case the least, in the centre will come number three. Behind the *toreros* will be their *banderilleros,* those responsible for placing the *banderillas* - the metre long, paper-decorated, steel barb-tipped darts.

Next in line are the rest of the *cuadrillas,* the team assistants. Each member is called a *peon* and they accompany the *torero* in the *plaza*. They're closely followed by the mounted *picadores,* whose job it is to weaken the bull by drawing first blood using the *vara* - the spear, by driving it into the nape known as the *morillo*. Alongside them are their assistants on foot called *monosabios* - wise monkeys, whose job with stick in hand it is to help maintain the *picador's* horse on its feet and as calm as possible. All those who enter in the *paseíllo* will have their moment of protagonism in the afternoon's drama. Behind the 'monkeys' appear the carpenters whose role it is to carry out makeshift repairs should the bull destroy any part of the wooden *barrera* that runs round the inner part of the ring. Accompanying them are those responsible for levelling the *albero* - the characteristic ochre sand floor of the ring, after each bull has been dealt with and which comes from the quarry of Álcala de Guadaira near Sevilla. Then, last to arrive are the harnessed mules adorned with bells and flags and their handlers right alongside. They will complete the act in the *plaza* by dragging away the defeated animal. With the parade over, the *toreros* and their *cuadrillas* set to work preparing capes and swords while the *alguaciles* in time-honoured fashion hand over the key to the tunnel that leads to the bull-pen - *los torriles,* in readiness for the bulls' entrance. All this takes place accompanied by the sound of the *plaza's* band, occupying an area high up among the crowd.

The spectators are arranged into its corresponding shadings. The *plaza* is uniquely divided into areas and levels, unlike any other theatre. The areas are: *sol, sol y sombra* and *sombra y sol. Sol* - 'Sun' are the cheapest seats owing to the hardship undertaken by the *aficionados* in the unforgiving rays. *Sol y sombra* seats enjoy a mixture of sun followed by shade as the star swings west, and the most expensive tickets are found here. The two levels that the *plaza* occupies are the *tendido* and *grada*. *El tendido* stretches from *la barrera,* at the ringside, up to the balcony area. High in *la grada* you may have a bird's eye view of things; but unfortunately us humans were never equipped with a bird's keen sight to fully appreciate such a vantage point. *La grada* is really only worthwhile if you are near the President's box and right up against the balustrade that runs the full length of the *plaza.* Otherwise, behind this parapet you really are in the cheap seats with pillars in the way, binoculars often required and conversation bouncing off the ceiling above.

The *paso doble,* which is played by the band to lend atmosphere to the scene, suddenly halts and the trumpet playing turns official. This signals the commencement of the first of the three *suertes* that constitute the act of killing a bull in a *plaza. (Suerte,* translates literally as 'luck' and it is another telling sign that such a word should be used to divide the *Corrida* into its constituent parts) The President hangs a white handkerchief over his balcony and the *torero* salutes him.

La puerta de los torriles - gate to the bull-pen, swings open and inside the depths of a tunnel waits a bull eager to escape its tight corral. As it stands bewildered, a ribbon bearing its breeder's colours, called a *divisa,* is spiked into its neck through the use of a long pole. Another gate slams open and anyone left in the ring runs for cover. Over 500kg of purebred glistening muscle on the hoof thunders out into the light in a rush of testosterone that overwhelms the dormant air hanging in the *plaza.*

The *peones* of the *cuadrilla* will draw the bull towards their *torero* by throwing out their heavy fuchsia-backed and yellow-lined capes as they hide behind one of four 'escape routes', called *burladeros,* protruding from the red, wooden barrier. Sometimes the *torero* will go out and kneel down in front of the *torril* from where the bull will issue forth. This is called a *larga cambiada de rodillas* or 'a long knee change', if such a translation is possible. It is also known as *'a porta gayola'*, which must surely translate as 'death wish' in any other language. If it is true that a woman wearing a stiletto heel applies the same pressure as an elephant then just imagine the force concentrated at the end of a bull's horn as it comes charging out with half a tonne weighing in behind it. Then take it one step further and imagine that horn catching you full in the face. Well, Franco Cordeño didn't have to imagine it... he experienced it, at first face. Although his visage was left hanging by a thread and his body half-emptied of life, he miraculously survived. His bar in Sevilla is called *'Porta Gayola'*. The local punters go there to get off their face as well.

A great part of the atmosphere of the *plaza* is the proximity of the arena. This was partly why the 1992 Barcelona Olympics were considered such a success. The crowd form part of the spectacle by being included in its proceedings and not separated from it. Once the bull is finally in the *plaza* the *torero* and his *cuadrilla* take over the reins. With their man-sized fuchsia serviettes they will play with the bull to determine which horn it tends to lead with. This is often the most colourful part of the three acts with all its dancing cape play. The long sweeps of the pink cloak - *capote*, are referred to as *veronicas*.

The three *suertes* are also known as *tercios* - thirds: 1) *La Suerte de Vara* 2) *La Suerte de Banderilla* 3) *La Suerte de Matar*. Each *suerte* or *tercio* sees the bull in one of these three stages as the theatre progresses. At first the bull's attitude is *levantado,* up for it. Then it is *parado,* slowed. Finally, it is *aplomado,* leaden or weighed down. The start of each *suerte* is signalled by the President draping a handkerchief from his balcony when the band sounds the change. A green handkerchief signals that the bull has to be returned and a *sobresaliente* - reserve bull, used. The indicating of the three *tercios* by the use of white handkerchief ensures that a time limit is adhered to. It takes an average of 15 minutes to kill a bull, in which period one hopes to witness spectacle and bravery while facing a possible fatality. For the first *suerte* the bull is fresh, unblemished by blood and the *torero* nowhere near a sword. This is the *Corrida* at its most vibrant, lucid and popular height, before things fundamentally change. Then the *torero* will draw the bull to the mounted *picador* who will thrust his spike into the back of the bull's neck in order to get the blood running. From here on in, things become more serious. The true nature of the meeting of man and beast in the arena becomes apparent. The red of blood replaces the red of the *fiesta.*

As tradition dictates, the *picador* must engage the bull twice and not enter the inner circle of the two marked rings in the sand. If he does, the crowd will let him know. He sits atop a gigantic Breton horse sporting protective padding called a *peta,* which was only introduced in 1928 under a Royal decree for fear of losing business from tourists. It stipulated that the maximum *peta* would weigh 30kg and the *picador's* horse a maximum of 650kg.

Before then the spectacle was appallingly bloody with bulls ripping through horses hides and leaving them gutted in the sand. Some were even sown up with their entrails crudely shoved back in place and sent out a second time. Hard to believe, but true. Goya's engravings in El Prado attest to this. Today the horses are padded and blindfolded but the internal damage done to these animals must still be great as the bull slams its pointed horns into its side with all the force and pace it can muster.

If the *picador* punishes the bull too much it will be too weak to complete the remaining two *suertes*. The balance is a fine one.

Some blood-letting is required, as without it the animal would take far too long to finish off. The *picador* retires along with a reserve *picador* positioned at the opposite end of the *plaza*.

The *torero* dedicates the bull by throwing his *montera* - hat, over his shoulder. Landing upside down is considered negative as superstition claims it will catch his spilt blood. If this should happen it is turned over. However, in this case some say that this will empty his luck. The glass here is either half-empty or half-empty, there seems to be no room for optimism. His bright heavy cape is exchanged for the smaller, familiar red *muleta* cape and the *espada* – sword. Another name for a *torero* is 'Espadas'. We enter the second *tercio: La Suerte de Banderillas,* in which a member of the *cuadrilla* will take on the bull by bearing his chest to it as he places three pairs of colourfully decorated barbed darts into the bull's considerable neck muscles. The handkerchief appears over the President's balcony and the *tercio* changes as we enter the third and fatal act: *La Suerte de Matar.*

The obvious risk-taking and blatant showmanship have come to an end. Now the real subtlety begins and the measure of the man's metal is demonstrated by his willingness to allow the bull closer and closer to his body. Who knows at what moment the bull will finally identify his enemy as the *torero* and leave the red *muleta* behind? More often than not this moment never comes, but when it does it is always too soon. This last *tercio, la suerte de matar,* is the moment of the famed *'¡Olé!'* when Spain's identity finds its voice in the exaltation that rings out across the stained

amphitheatre. This is also when the *torero* will decide whether to close the distance between his safety and that of mortal danger. In so doing he will intensify the brittle line between his existence and own extinction. It is what the true *aficionado* has come to feel, more than see.

The atmosphere always calms at this point, maybe as a mark of respect, or maybe because nothing poignant will happen until the sword goes in. The *torero* returns to the *barrera* and changes his straight sword for a curved one, handed to him by his helper known as *mozo de espadas,* so shaped to ensure an arched entrance into the bull's body. It is the *torero's* decision as to when he will go to the *barrera* to change his sword and take the act into its final stage by lining the bull up for the kill. The change of sword for the *estoque* is needed because the one he has been using up until then is blunt, so as not to cut himself. Permission is finally asked to kill the bull and formally given by the President.

Sometimes the bull's sacrifice is dedicated as the band plays a *paso doble.* Then he will pass the bull a few times with the cape until he places the animal where he wants it. Taking up position he will dip the cape to the ground. This will lower the bull's head thereby exposing its nape, *el morillo.* The sword is lifted high as the *torero* peers down it like a sniper taking aim between the bull's shoulder blades, and in almost one movement he jerks the cape over the bull's eyes, lets out a grunt of provocation as the bull hooks its neck forward to charge. The *torero* leans the sword into its target and in an instant there is a flash of *torero,* cape, sword, bull, sash, sequins, steel and blood-soaked hide. The onlookers wait for the confused parts to separate so they can make out where the sword and *torero* have ended up and what, if any, is the immediate response of the bull.

If the final blow, *la estocada,* has been dealt deep enough it should be a matter of only a few moments before the bull vomits blood. When it falls to the ground a *peon* will cut its spinal cord in the back of the neck, bringing an end to its life. Sometimes the sword is poorly placed and has to be thrust in again until it strikes home. Sometimes the blade is simply left there and the *peones* move in with their fuchsia capes, one on either side of the bull, flicking them in turn to make the bull move from side to side. This is to enable the sword to splice through more veins and arteries to bring the animal to its knees. The longer this takes the more the audience will whistle and jeer the *torero*. While hungry to see the kill they are angered to see the suffering drag on. If this fails to finish the *faena,* another sword with a crosspiece close to the tip, called *descabello* is taken from the *barrera* and used to sever the bull's spinal cord. This is done while the bull stands motionless. A quick jab behind the neck usually sees the bull jerk and drop dead. The moment this occurs a *banderillero* will stab a small knife, *puntilla,* into the same place delivering a *coup de grâce.*

With the snap of the nerves and the last rigid twitch of the bull's torso, it is over. The audience will applaud before it has its spinal cord severed if the animal falls to its knees soon after the sword goes in. They know that the *torero* has timed things right and the bull had had little left in him. The *torero,* delighted to see his foe felled and his own limbs still intact, will skip round the arena with a youthful step and play out a social rite of the ring, which has infiltrated the imagination of the wider Spanish people. The man will go out to the centre of the ring or a place where he stands alone and draw in the attention of the crowd, holding out his arm with a flat palm extended and then slowly turn full circle giving a peculiar pirouette salute and tribute to the people. More often than not he will finish off by wrapping both arms around himself and the hugging formality symbolising his bond of friendship and admiration for those who chant the three syllable adulation of the ring: *'to-**RE**-ro, to-*

RE-*ro'*. These motifs, very much from the ring, are found in everyday Spanish society, from the pop artist waving the audience and Almodóvar receiving his Oscar, to someone scoring a goal or a man being heckled by a group of girls. Those who receive a Spanish crowd's adulation will often hear the chant '*to*-**RE**-*ro*' at some stage in the applause, whether it be at the theatre or on a game show.

While the *torero* moves back to the *barrera* or *tablas* to drink water and store the sword, the crowd hold up their white handkerchiefs signalling the President to award the *torero* an ear, two ears or both ears and the tail. The importance of this will later be reflected in the annual 'rankings'. The more ears - *orejas,* he receives the higher up the ladder he is and the greater the demand for his services will be come the next round of billings for the national *fiesta*. If the President holds out the handkerchief once he concedes an ear, twice two ears and if three times the *matador de toros* is granted both ears and the tail - *el rabo*. The trophies are cut then and there from the bull and handed over. The *torero* will give another characteristic salute and possibly throw the ears and tail into the crowd.

If the *torero* achieves ears when killing both bulls of the afternoon and brings a quick, successful kill after having brought the spectacle to a fever of excitement, then he is carried shoulder-high through the main gates at the close of the *Corrida*. This is called '*salir por la puerta grande*' - 'to go out through the great door', similar to the common phrase we use: 'going out with style', but the Spanish phrase also carries the added meaning that you are carried on the shoulders of others for the ecstatic moment you have given them. As bullrings are divided into three classes, each will stipulate its own criteria for when a *torero* is carried out and it usually depends on the number of ears he has cut during the afternoon. In Sevilla the greatest accolade that one may receive is to be carried out through *La Puerta de Príncipes,* where the press and jubilant masses await.

Los toreros are supposed to be *otra raza* - another breed, and as such, they are often revered in Spain. This is believed to be because of their ability to face the bull again after having been seriously gored. Some try to stand up and finish the job while others need immediate surgical intervention and will have to wait out their months of recovery before they can face a pair of horns again. *'El torero es otra raza'* is a phrase that you will often hear.

Madrid and its *plaza, Las Ventas* is the Mecca of *Los Toros* and its *Feria de San Isidro* its time of high pilgrimage, even though Andalucía is the birthplace of the art form. For many though, to triumph in *'La Maestranza'* - *La Plaza de Toros de Sevilla,* is the most sublime moment that the confrontation between bull and man may bring. *Las Ventas* in Madrid may be the most important, but it is *La Maestranza* in Sevilla where all Spanish *toreros* wish to triumph at least once in their careers.

For the visiting tourist the biggest pull is probably the social event itself, which is infectious and what the majority of the Spanish bullwatchers equally enjoy. In Seville the afternoon starts with people mingling in bars sipping *fino* or *manzanilla* wine, striped cushions, unique to the arena, swing nonchalantly from people's hands. Fine dresses, jackets and ties outnumber jeans and T-shirts in and around *calle Adriano* behind the bullring. Horse-drawn carriages pull up and *señoritas*, who will be seated conspicuously in *la Grada* near the *puerta de los Príncipes*, step down sporting laced *mantillas* cascading from ornamental high comb *peinetas*. The area around the entrance, giving out onto the Guadalquivir River, is awash with horses and carriages bringing owners and friends from the city's April Fair - *la Feria de abril,* where flamenco is played, families gather and everyone dances *sevillanas*. Traffic is diverted and crowds gather to see Spain's high, and not so high, society parade in. Cameras are suspended over the cobbled entrance to get a glimpse of a popular face and there are plenty about. The atmosphere is bathed in the bright sunshine and in the blue sky the flags of Spain, Andalucía and the *Real Maestranza* flutter floridly. Everyone wears sunglasses for practical and impractical reasons. Mobile phones and other fashion accessories are similarly evident. The scenario oozes old money and newly made fortunes eager to rub shoulders. Havana smoke fills the air and Cuban *aficionados* are two-a-penny. It is the society scene *Sevilla* style.

You don't get in cheap either and an *abono* - season ticket, for example in prime position for the 2004 bullfight season in *Tendido 1, Barrera, 1° Fila,* for: "*19 Corridas de Toros, 2 Corridas del Arte del Rejoneo y 8 Novilladas con Picadores*" weighed in at a hefty €2,745. The cheapest was €428 in the *Grada Especial.*

Britain's representatives in the ring can be counted on three fifths of a hand; there have been just three of them. In the 1950's there was the extravagant ex-public school type Vincent Hitchcock, whose autobiography is *'Suit of Lights'.* Then in the 1960's there was Henry Higgins who met his end in the

Almerian town of Mojácar in 1978 caught by a bull in its *plaza*. His autobiography is *'To Be a Matador'*. He is buried in the town's cemetery. Then in the 1970's came Frank Evans known as *'El Inglés'* and Fran to his Spanish friends. At the tender of age of 17, in 1966, he faced his first bull and as recently as the year 2000, he was still in the ring. He didn't make the big time despite paying the penultimate sacrifice in 1984 when a bull caught him from behind, in the bull's eye you could say. As yet he hasn't written an autobiography. He'll probably get round to it the moment he can sit down at a writing desk. Since then there have been three others rising through the ranks and at the time of writing there was even a 14-year-old girl known as *La Holly*.

There is of course one last question to be asked after the long hot afternoon draws to a close and the people make their way out of the *plaza* and into the bars to wax lyrical, take *tapas* and drink a few lazy hours away. What happens to the bull? The meat is sold on. Highly prized it is too, though strangely not of the highest quality. The tail finds its way into the best restaurants where *cola de toro* is considered a delicacy. The testicles are also highly prized but it has not been conclusively decided whether or not their properties can be passed on through ingestion. The well-worn *Corrida* anecdote breathes new life each time it finds an innocent tourist's ear and goes something like this: An American goes into a restaurant and asks for bull's testicles, *testículos de toro,* and when he is presented with the dish he remarks on their extremely small size. The waiter leans in close and whispers, *"Sometimes señor... the bull wins."*

Michael Palin said something quite poignant about the subject in his video *'Hemingway Adventures'*, which would make a fitting end for this, the oldest of Spanish themes:

"For me it's a Spanish thing. I will never feel about it the way they do. And that alone intrigues me."

OLD SEVILLE

- *The City of Eternal Youth* -

Florence has its glorious architecture, Egypt its ancient foundations, Rio de Janeiro its carnival, New Orleans its music, Pamplona its festivities, Istanbul is a bi-continental crossroads and Rome and London were once centres of world Empire. All of this is captured in Spain in just one city: Seville.

What other city can lay such a claim?

But how much do we know of Seville compared to the others? It is time to redress the balance and discover a city loved by all that have visited her. Seville was founded by Hercules and built by the Phoenicians. She was the second city of Imperial Rome and then blossomed to become second to none when she discovered another world. Seville is home of the humble '*tapa*', the Inquisition, the bullfight, a cornerstone of Flamenco, a city that inspired and spawned Carmen, Don Giovanni, Figaro, the Barber of and where Christopher Columbus rests in the world's biggest gothic cathedral. This is the city that took baseball and cowboys to the New World, set Magellan off around the world and welcomed his boats back. It was an African capital in Europe, whose exotic Moorish monuments attest to. It went on to bridge Europe and the Americas to become the 'New York' of its day.

There are few cultures that kick up their heels like Spain and there is certainly no Spanish city more *alegre* than Seville. It made a lasting impression on the likes of Byron, Borrow, Brenan and all of the great Hispanophiles. When one imagines the temperamental fantasy of Spain one is thinking exclusively of Seville and her legacy. Its glorious past is mirrored by its vibrant present and infectious atmosphere. London, New York and Paris may be on cigarette packets and shopping bags but Seville is found in writers' eulogies and engrained in the visitors' imagination.

Seville is the fame and fable of all things Spanish. Hence, if you don't know Seville you will never fathom Spain. While *Sevilla* has been largely forgotten since it discovered the New World its citizens still believe their world spins at the centre of the old universe. It's just waiting for you to rediscover it and see why they just might be right.

website:

https://thehispanophileseries.wordpress.com

Instagram:

the_hispanophile

Made in the USA
Las Vegas, NV
27 March 2021